Savvy

WRITER'S NOTEBOOK

# CATCH YOUR BREATH

## Writing Poignant Poetry

by Laura Purdie Salas

**CAPSTONE PRESS**

a capstone imprint

**Savvy Books are published by Capstone Press,**
**1710 Roe Crest Drive, North Mankato, Minnesota 56003**
www.capstonepub.com

All poems used with permission.

Library of Congress Cataloging-in-Publication Data
Salas, Laura Purdie.
Catch your breath : writing poignant poetry / by Laura Purdie Salas
pages cm.—(Savvy writer's notebook)
Includes bibliographical references and index.
Summary: "Introduces and defines essential elements of writing poetry accompanied by compelling writing prompts for practicing new skills. Real-life author bios and excerpts enhance skills and understanding"-- Provided by publisher.
ISBN 978-1-4914-5990-4 (library binding : alk. paper) -- ISBN 978-1-4914-5994-2 (pbk. : alk. paper) -- ISBN 978-1-4914-5998-0 (ebook pdf)
1. Poetry--Authorship--Juvenile literature. 2. Creative writing--Juvenile literature.  I. Title. PN1059.A9S344 2015
 808.1--dc23 2015015333

Editorial Credits
Jeni Wittrock, editor; Veronica Scott, designer; Morgan, media researcher; Katy LaVigne, production specialist

Photo Credits
AP Images: Tina Fineberg, 10; Getty Images: Ilya Dreyvitser/Stringer, (nikki) top left 45; Shutterstock: 29september, 25, Anuka, 24, Artex67, 56, Cat Rocketship, 42, crazystocker, 4, Elise Gravel, Cover, isaxar, 27, Iya Khrakovsky, 61, jumpingsack, 31, kasha_malasha, 53, Kira Culufin, 60, KUCO, 9, Kudryashka, 59, Le Do, 41, Legend_tp, 36, Lightspring, 58, lolya1988, (leaf background) 17, makar, 18, Marina Giniatulina, 47, Markovka, (sea creatures) 14-15, Michele Paccione, (cat prints) 17, Mrs. Opossum, 29, Natalia Hubbert, 37, natalia_maroz, 38, 39, 46, Nazar Yosyfiv, 7, 21, npine, 44, 51, Olga1818, 49, Ollyy, 13, Paisit Teeraphatsakool, 45, Phil McDonald, 16, Pshenina_m, 22, sarsmis, 19, schatzy, 32, Sergey Nivens, 5, Sergey Peterman, 35, Steve Cukrov, 23, Stmool, 52, Taweepat, (notebook & pens) 45, Valery Sidelnykov, 54, Yu Zhang, 11, zhuk.alyona, 8, 12, Zita, 55; Wikimedia: Brittany.lynk/Sonya Sones, 43, Deerstop, 33, Slp1, 20

Printed in the United States of America in North Mankato, Minnestoa.
062015        008823CGF15

# TABLE OF CONTENTS

# Introduction

"Writing poetry is taking a subject—be it a pigeon or a Popsicle—and breathing new life into it."

—Lee Bennett Hopkins, author of City I Love, Mary's Song, and more, and a Guinness World Records anthologist

If you want a definition, poetry is words broken into lines instead of paragraphs. But as a writer, you know poetry is much more than that. Poets create striking images that plant themselves in a reader's brain. They combine words in surprising, unexpected ways. Poets can show readers something new—or something old, but in a new way. Good poetry makes readers' minds blossom!

# Chapter 1

# The Poetry Habit

Poets have limitless imaginations. They're often quirky and love to observe things in their own unique way. When they look at a crow, for instance, they might think of a scoop of licorice ice cream or a splash of oil. Poets love to pinpoint just the right words to describe things. They often love music, and that includes the sounds of letters and words. They can be very particular about the way a poem looks on the page.

Does this sound like you? Congratulations, you're a poet!

Poets write poetry. No surprise there. But there are habits (besides just "sit down and write") that can make you an even better poet.

# Habit 1: Embrace

Poets tend to think a little differently and feel things really deeply. And that's a good thing. For instance, read how Kate Coombs describes her relationship with poetry—in a poem called "Poems."

i.
it's time to sleep
but the poems
lope up my spine howling
like I'm their moon.

ii.
it's time to sleep
but the poems
inventory my dreams
like pinball machines.

iii.
it's time to sleep
but the poems come
waving their eyestalks
like metaphors
swinging their spider legs,
pittering their lavender feet.

iv.
the poems come
flipping the world like a pancake
flipping the world
the way water flips light.

–Kate Coombs, "Poems," author of *Water Sings Blue*,
*The Runaway Princess*, and more, all rights reserved

Coombs' phrases are unusual, right? That's exactly what makes them memorable! Her passion for language, image, and music comes through loud and clear. Poets embrace offbeat words and phrases, and they dig deeper into their emotions. You can bet no two poets will express an experience in the exact same way. Indeed, it is a poet's individual spin on the world that makes poems special and unique.

YOUR TURN

Coombs describes poetry as something that invades her life and turns her world upside down. What picture comes to your mind when you think of the word "poetry"? A silver stream that makes you calm and relaxed? A booming concert that makes you want to dance? A high-power microscope to study something in detail?

Write a poem that brings poetry to life. You might want to describe how a poem moves, what it eats or thinks, what it wears, and more.

# Habit 2: Read More to Write Better

Athletes watch other athletes perform. They study what works and what doesn't. They see what techniques have been tried and what techniques they want to use. This same approach works for writing poetry.

To become a better poet, you've got to start reading poetry. In fact, read lots of it—old poetry, new poetry, rhyming, and non-rhyming. Read library books, song lyrics, literary journals, and whatever else you can get your hands on. Make poetry part of your daily life.

When you find a poem you love, read it again. Do certain words or phrases surprise you? Is the poem fun to read aloud? Jot down your thoughts using sticky notes or a notebook. Save a copy of the poem and highlight your favorite words and lines. You could even make a handmade book of your favorite poems.

Of course, you won't like every poem you read. However, even a poem you don't particularly like may have lessons for you. Why don't you like it? Is it too long? Is it boring? Is it confusing? Think about what you don't like in poems, and work to avoid those qualities in your own poetry.

**YOUR TURN**

Studying other poets' work will strengthen your own writing skills, so hit up your local library for some fresh poetry books. While you're there, create a book-spine poem. Browse the shelves and pull out books with interesting titles. Then try stacking books so the titles on the spines form a poem when read from top to bottom. Take a picture of your book-spine poem to share with friends.

# AUTHOR PROFILE:

## Thanhha Lai

Advice to young writers: "Read what you like, not because it's popular. Read it because you feel something. It's from feeling something that you're going to produce your own work."

–Thanhha Lai

Thanhha Lai was born in Vietnam in the 1960s. While her father was fighting in the Vietnam War (1959–1975), her mother worked to support the family. At the end of the war, in 1975, her family moved to Alabama. Lai wrote a novel in verse based on the culture shock of that move. *Inside Out & Back Again* won a National Book Award.

## from "American Address"

Mother's face crinkles
like paper on fire.
She tells Brother Quang
to clamp shut his mouth.

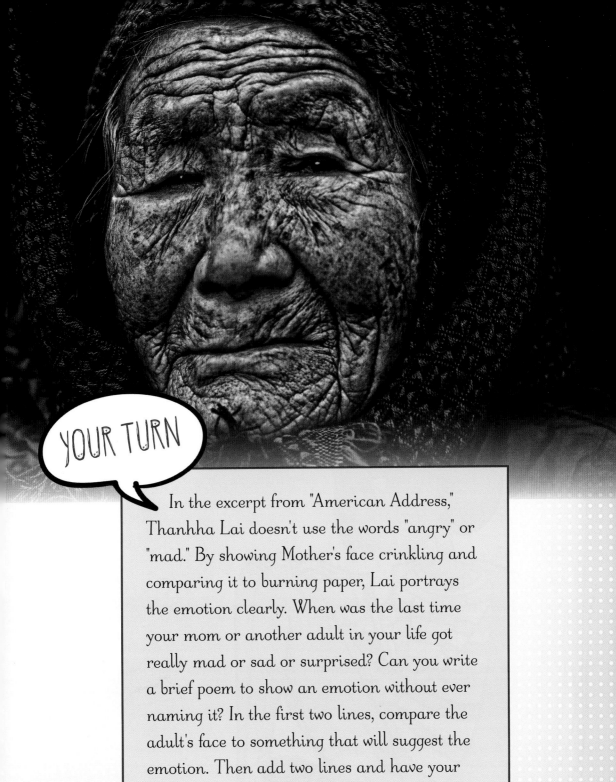

**YOUR TURN**

In the excerpt from "American Address," Thanhha Lai doesn't use the words "angry" or "mad." By showing Mother's face crinkling and comparing it to burning paper, Lai portrays the emotion clearly. When was the last time your mom or another adult in your life got really mad or sad or surprised? Can you write a brief poem to show an emotion without ever naming it? In the first two lines, compare the adult's face to something that will suggest the emotion. Then add two lines and have your adult take action that also shows the emotion.

# Habit 3: Don't Lose Your Ideas

Every writer knows that the best ideas pop up at totally random times—in the shower, on the bus, or in the hallway at school. Like shooting stars, your brightest ideas can appear out of nowhere, and they disappear equally fast!

Don't lose your ideas—keep an idea notebook. Or, if you prefer, stash your ideas in a folder. You can use almost anything from a memo phone app to a fish bowl to an empty donut bucket. No matter where you keep them, gather and save those fleeting, glittering ideas before they're gone.

# Chapter 2

# So Many Choices!

Pop, hip-hop, dubstep, orchestral—there are lots of styles of music. Similarly, there are many types of poems. There are rhyming poems, of course. But poems don't have to rhyme. Some poems don't rhyme and don't seem to have any obvious rules at all. Those poems are called free verse. Coombs' poem "Poems" is an example of free verse. But other non-rhyming poems have specific forms, each with its own rules. Try a few. You'll probably find that the limitations of poetry forms push your creativity and add an extra goal or challenge to the writing process.

If you aren't feeling one form, try another! Just like music, you'll probably find that some forms can move you, while others might leave you shaking your head. Which form will you take to? There's only one way to find out.

# Found Poem

## (So Easy It Feels Like Cheating—But It's Not)

A found poem borrows words or short phrases from something already published, such as a newspaper article or speech, to make a poem. The result might be enchanting, funny, or dark—and it will probably sound different from the poems you usually write. If you feel like you're always writing in the same style, a found poem will help ease you out of your comfort zone.

To try writing a poem that makes use of someone else's words, a magazine or newspaper is a good place to start. Make a copy or print-out of something that grabs you. As you read, highlight the words and phrases that you like. Play with, narrow down, and rearrange your chosen words to create a poem. As long as it's not exactly word for word, and you don't use more than 100 or so words, it is considered fair use.

Poet David Harrison read a travel article about a French food trend of adding seaweed (long used by Japanese chefs) to different foods. He chose words from that article to create a whimsical poem about food and culture.

# JUST ADD ALGAE

You'll find algae
in your bread near
Luxemburg Gardens.

Blame it on
the Japanese.

The hot French thing?
Developing a taste
for seaweed,
briny but delicate,
adding layers of flavors.

Sea bass slices,
raw oysters,
three kinds of algae . . .

Developing a taste
for seaweed,
that sushi staple?
Blame it on
the Japanese.

–David L. Harrison, author of *Pirates,
Cowboys*, and more, all rights reserved

Found poem source: "Just Add Algae,"
*Condé Nast Traveler*, June 2010

# Haiku

## (Short and Seasonal)

A haiku is a short poem that captures a moment in nature. Today's American haiku form is based on an old Japanese form. The American haiku usually has 3 lines. Many poets stick to a 5-7-5 syllable count. That means line 1 has 5 syllables, line 2 has 7, and line 3 has 5. The word "whispers" has two syllables: whis-pers. The word "together" has three: to-ge-ther. "New" is a one-syllable word. Saying a word out loud while you clap to each syllable can make it easier to hear the syllables.

Here's a modern haiku using the strict syllable count:

spring wind whispers by
birches gossip together
new leaves coming soon

Some poets ignore the syllable count. They just focus on writing a brief poem that precisely shows one single moment in nature.

## Here's an example of that kind of haiku.

autumn wind
the cat in a frenzy
chasing leaves

## YOUR TURN

To begin, head outside and look around. Find some action, such as squirrels playing or a shadow moving. Then write four traditional 5-7-5 haiku, one for each season. Make sure a word in each haiku shows the season. And that the haiku relates to the action.

# Acrostic

## (Read Down, Then Across)

Lively
Acrobatic
Understanding
Respectful
Amazing

    Did you ever have to write your name down your paper and then come up with words to describe yourself that started with each letter? That's an acrostic!

    Acrostics can be entertaining—and challenging! The trick is to pick words that delight, surprise, feel natural, and start with the right letter. Check out the next acrostic by a poet who loves everything about Christmas—except one particular food.

# UNWANTED GUEST

Blessings
Upon
This

Wintery
Holiday!
Yuletide's

Twinkling
Hours--
Even

Flying
Reindeer!—
Utterly
Irresistible
Turkey

Cranberries
Apple pie
Knockout
Eggnog . . .

What holiday do you love? Can you think of one tiny part of it that you don't love (like the fruitcake)? Write an acrostic about it. Do you notice that fruitcake is not mentioned in the poem "Unwanted Guest"? Only readers who realize it's an acrostic will get the reward of the answer being spelled out. Try not to use the word that you spell out in the body of your poem.

## AUTHOR PROFILE:

### Adelaide Crapsey

Adelaide Crapsey was a literature and poetry professor who died of tuberculosis at 36 years old. Crapsey loved Japanese forms like haiku, and she invented the cinquain. This form shares some characteristics of haiku, with its compressed language and strict structure. Here's one of Crapsey's cinquains.

## NIAGARA

(Seen on a Night in November )
How frail
Above the bulk
Of crashing water hangs,
Autumnal, evanescent, wan,
The moon.

–by Adelaide Crapsey, poem in the public domain

# Cinquain

## (2, 4, 6, 8, 2 Do We Appreciate?)

A cinquain is a non-rhyming form. It always has five lines of 2, 4, 6, 8, and 2 syllables. Generally cinquains rely on sensory description to paint a scene and make the reader feel a certain mood.

**YOUR TURN**

Take a shot at writing a cinquain inspired by the image on this page. Sometimes the first or last line names the topic of the poem. In Crapsey's cinquain, you don't know until the final line that the topic is the moon. In a longer poem, this might be irritating, but it works fine in a short form like this. It builds up suspense. If you like that effect, try revealing your topic in the last 2-syllable line, and use the first four lines to describe or hint at it.

# Fibonacci

## (Good, Honest Fun)

Here's an unusual poetic form: a Fibonacci. The Fibonacci sequence is a pattern that occurs in nature in nautilus shells, waves, pine cones, and more. The pattern is this: each row equals the sum of the two rows before.

A six-line Fibonacci poem has syllable counts of 1, 1, 2, 3, 5, and 8. To make powerful Fibs, leave out lazy words, such as "the" and "a," when possible. Fill your Fibs with strong verbs and specific nouns. Here's a slightly disgusting Fib!

Cat
heaves:
hair ball.
Hork hork hork.
What a squicky noise.
Cleanup needed in upstairs hall!

Fibonaccis can be as long as you want. But be warned. If you write a 10-line Fib, that last line will have 55 syllables! The topic is open, so this is an opportunity to try something random. Here's an idea: Grab a paint chip (a sample) at the hardware store. Use the name of the paint color as the title and topic for your Fibonacci. In case you don't have access to a hardware store, here are three paint color names to choose from:

American Cheese

Plum Perfect

Potter's Wheel

# Chapter 3

# To Rhyme or Not to Rhyme

## Rhyming Is Harder Than It Looks

Some people's favorite poems are song lyrics. Lyrics usually rhyme, and a lot of young writers want to write rhyming poems too. Unfortunately, an idea for a rhyming poem that sounds great in your head might be disappointing when you get it down on paper. Creating meaningful, original rhymes is no easy task.

Why is excellent, natural-sounding, interesting verse so hard to write? Here are a few common pitfalls:

- Many poets read aloud well and auto-correct their own rhythm problems without realizing it. The word "going," for example, has the accent on the "go" syllable. But a poet who is rhyming "going" with "spring" might pronounce it as "goING."

- Rhyme takes over meaning, resulting in nonsense or overused words. If you write a rhyming poem about a girl who skis, and you mention that she has fleas, your reader will know that you put that in just for the rhyme. Try to make your rhymes sound natural—like it's a coincidence that the perfect words for your poem happen to rhyme!

- Focusing on rhyme and rhythm and ignoring other elements such as metaphor and imagery (using words related to the senses to create a world for your reader). That results in a less interesting poem.

- Filler words like "oh," "so," and "and" water down many rhyming poems.

So now you know why rhyme is challenging. But if you're wild for rhyme, attack it and have fun with it.

# Three Kinds of Rhyme

All rhyme is not equal. There are three different kinds. Perfect rhyme is traditional rhyme. "Skis" and "fleas" are perfect rhymes. Then there's near rhyme, which is when you use words with similar sounds at the ends of lines. "Woods," "good," and "foot" are near rhymes. And, finally, there's internal rhyme. That's when perfect rhyme is used inside lines instead of at the end. You'll see that in the poem "Body Art," where "speckles" and "freckles" are internal rhymes.

All these types of rhyme are great. It's just a matter of consistency. If you use perfect rhyme in 90 percent of your poem, you can't use near rhyme in 10 percent. It's always obvious and jarring to the reader. In that case, it's best to choose a whole new pair of rhyming words.

## Find the Beat

Besides good rhyme, you need good meter, or rhythm. Your meter is the pattern of your accented syllables (the ones you emphasize or say a little louder) and your unaccented syllables (the ones you do not say louder). Mark your syllables to see the pattern—and where you've broken it.

Start with the last line on your poem, and read it aloud as if it's just a normal sentence. Highlight or make the accented syllables all capitals. Repeat, moving up, line by line, through your poem. Then look for the patterns.

In this example, the capitalized syllables show where one reader emphasized the sound. The number of accented beats is in parentheses after each line.

## MISSING HUE

When GRASS is ALL done GROWing,                          (3)

and it's NOT yet TIME for SNOWing,                        (3)

there's a NEITHer/ALmost SEAson IN beTWEEN               (5)

when LEAVES turn BROWN and WRINKly,                       (3)

and they TWIRL to EARTH all CRINKly.                      (3)

Every FALL, i WONder WHAT beCAME of GREEN.               (5)

Read the poem out loud, and clap on the capitalized syllables. Do you hear the rhythm? If this feels difficult to you, don't worry. Every poet who has ever written a good rhyming poem has written at least 100 bad ones! Keep working on rhyme, but spend time on free verse or non-rhyming forms, too. That way you'll challenge yourself but also produce poems you're really proud of!

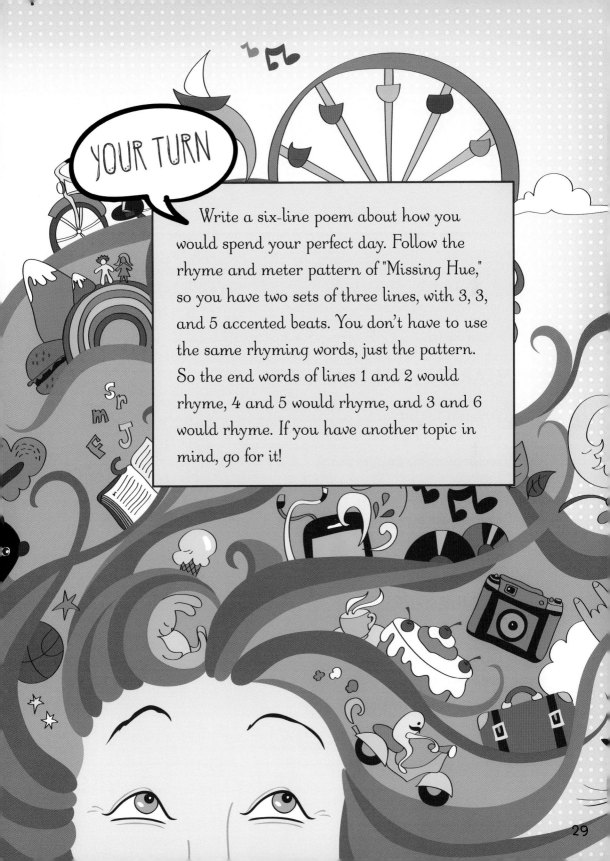

YOUR TURN

Write a six-line poem about how you would spend your perfect day. Follow the rhyme and meter pattern of "Missing Hue," so you have two sets of three lines, with 3, 3, and 5 accented beats. You don't have to use the same rhyming words, just the pattern. So the end words of lines 1 and 2 would rhyme, 4 and 5 would rhyme, and 3 and 6 would rhyme. If you have another topic in mind, go for it!

# When the Little Words Are Very, Very Boring

Poetry's strength lies in its concentration of images and details in very few words. Filler words like "a," "very," and "so" tend to weaken poems. As you write, try to stuff every single line full of as much detail and content as possible. Don't waste your space with meaningless words like "and then" or "very, very."

## GARAGE SALE JEANS

Who was the kid
who wore you before
you became my favorite jeans?

You had a shell
in your back pocket.
I wonder what it means.

I wish I could
meet that old kid
who wore you long ago.

Garage sale jeans
keep secrets
new owners never know.

–Amy Ludwig VanDerwater, author of *Forest Has a Song*, all rights reserved

**YOUR TURN**

What's in your closet that used to be someone else's? Do you have a vintage skirt? Hand-me-downs from an older sister? A boyfriend's jacket? Choose a single item and write a rhyming poem with three-line stanzas. Remember to weed out those meaningless little words.

# When Out of Order Are the Words

When rhyming, try to make your phrasing sound natural. For instance, this does not sound natural:

No one answered when he knocked,
so to the store he slowly walked.

Nobody says, "to the store he slowly walked." They say, "He slowly walked to the store." When you move the verb to the end, it's a neon arrow pointing at the problem. You want your poem to seem effortless, but inverted word order lets your reader see you sweat.

Read aloud as you write. Your lines should feel fairly natural to say. Ask yourself, "Would my friends look at me like I had grown an extra head if I said this in a conversation?" If the answer's yes, check to see if inverted word order is the problem. If the verb comes before the subject, it's inverted. It's also inverted if a phrase that gives more detail about the verb comes before the verb. This is the case in the above example: "to the store" would come after "he slowly walked" in normal conversation.

## AUTHOR PROFILE:

### Emily Dickinson

Emily Dickinson was a 19th-century Massachusetts poet. Even though she lived a solitary life, she wrote often of love and loss. She wrote almost 1,800 poems, mostly rhyming. Dickinson's first poetry book wasn't published until after her death, but today she is considered one of the creators of uniquely American poetry.

## A BOOK.

He ate and drank the precious words,
His spirit grew robust;
He knew no more that he was poor,
Nor that his frame was dust.
He danced along the dingy days,
And this bequest of wings
Was but a book. What liberty
A loosened spirit brings!

–by Emily Dickinson, poem in the public domain

### YOUR TURN

Quick! Grab your cell phone or some other favorite tech device. Write a rhyming poem that tells about the wonderful things that everyday object does for you.

# Chapter 4

# Poetry Building Blocks

## Ready to Cook Up a Poem

A good chef uses many basic ingredients all the time—salt, sugar, flour, etc. She turns them into everything from pancakes to pot pies. It's the same with poetry. There are some basic great poetry ingredients that you will use to cook up your best poems, whether they are rhyming, free verse, or specific forms.

## Can You Smell It?

Poems need sensory language—words related to your five senses. And don't settle for just sight words (shiny, burgundy, towering). Also work in textures (bumpy, feathery, soft), smells (bleach, cinnamon, wet dog), and sounds (crack!, meow, sob) and even tastes (salt, chlorine, tangy). Sensory words make the difference between:

Her backpack was stuffed with books and papers.

   and

Crumpled papers spilled from the musty green backpack in Lost and Found.

Sensory language makes poems unique and memorable. Here are a few lines from "Something Told the Wild Geese" by Rachel Field:

All the sagging orchards
Steamed with amber spice,
But each wild breast stiffened
At remembered ice.

In that excerpt, Field uses words that call to mind movement (sagging, stiffened), temperature (steamed, ice), color (amber), smell (spice), and texture (wild breast—goose feathers—and ice). Masterful!

**YOUR TURN**

Sensory words put your reader right there into your poem. They help your reader live the experience you're writing about. Choose three to five sensory words used in the backpack sentence or the poem excerpt. Use them to inspire a free verse poem—and add more sensory words too!

# Comparisons

## (But a Bus Is NOT Like a Puppy!)

Comparison is a key ingredient is many poems. Metaphors and similes both compare two unlike things. But they do it in different ways. Metaphors say that one thing is another thing.

## HOW IS A MEADOW AN OCEAN?

A meadow's an ocean with wild waves of wheat
Thunder's a drummer that's keeping storm's beat

A bus is a puppy that runs down the street
A desk is a robot with round, metal feet

A metaphor's a window that changes our view,
A gift to unwrap, something old made brand new

--Laura Purdie Salas, all rights reserved

Each line in that poem contains a metaphor. A bus is not really like a puppy! Still, the comparison can help you see a bus in a new way. By calling a bus "a puppy that runs down the street," the poem makes the bus seem eager and friendly. But if you were writing about the worst bus ride of your life, maybe you'd write, "A bus is a jail cell with seats of concrete." The comparison should tell your reader how to feel about the object.

Similes also compare two unlike things. They do that using the word "like" or "as."

The announcement sawed **like** a knife at my spine
Tulips were **like** yellow buckets, catching the rain

Kate Coombs' poem says that poems flip the world "like a pancake." That's a simile.

**YOUR TURN**

Write a rhyming list poem about your bedroom, using metaphors and/or similes. Try to avoid comparing your bedroom to other kinds of rooms. Compare it to things that are completely different.

# Repetition
# Repetition

We tend to repeat important things and things we like. Peek in your closet. Do you see lots of stripes? Or mostly red? That repetition shows something about you.

It's the same in a poem. Repetition emphasizes important words or phrases. It tells the reader, "Pay attention!" Repetition also enhances the musicality of a poem. That's the feeling of words sounding wonderful, with flows and pauses in all the right places. Look at "but the poems" in the Kate Coombs' poem. This repeated phrase does both of these jobs.

YOUR TURN

Write a free verse poem about yourself called "I Will Be ..." You might share what you want to be next week (nice to your little brother?) or in 10 years (a scientist?). Repeat the phrase "I will be" at least three times. Here's a sample beginning:

## WHEN I MOVE...

I will be me
    designing sets for Theater Club
    cartwheeling to the mailbox
    watching my nightlight flicker at midnight

I will be someone new
    who didn't face-plant on the asphalt in P.E.
    whose mom didn't yell at the PTA meeting
    who doesn't get sick from the smell of green beans

—Laura Purdie Salas, all rights reserved

# Alliteration, Assonance, and Consonance: Making Sounds Sound Fun

A begging beagle. A thick vanilla milkshake. A sweater of fur and feathers. The way words sound together is an important element of poetry. Playing with sounds will make your poem more pleasing to the ear.

Alliteration is when a sound is repeated at the start of several words (like the /b/ sounds in "begging beagle"). Assonance is a repeated vowel sound inside words—like the three /i/ sounds in "thick vanilla milkshake." And consonance is a repeated consonant sound inside words—like the /r/ sounds in "sweater of feathers and fur."

Can you find the alliteration and assonance in this haiku?

## ABANDONMENT

Sparrow sweetly sings
melancholy melody;
her mate, on the ground.

—Matt Forrest Esenwine, all rights reserved

40

Here's another poem that uses repeated sounds. This is a triolet—an eight-line poem with a certain pattern of rhyme and meter. As you read it, what consonant sound do you notice repeated in the first three lines?

Hawks circle fields and furrows,
slicing spirals in the sky.
Field mice scurry into burrows.
Hawks circle fields and furrows,
keeping watch for shifting shadows
seeking spots where field mice hide.
Hawks circle fields and furrows
slicing spirals in the sky.

Did you hear the /er/ sound in circle, furrows, scurry, and burrows? And the /k/ sound in Hawks, circle, sky, and scurry? Those are examples of consonance.

# Chapter 5

# What Should You Write About?

## When You're Short on Ideas

What if you're ready to write a poem but the words won't come? Take American writer Jack London's advice: "Don't loaf and invite inspiration; light out after it with a club . . ."

That's right—you need to jump down a poem's throat and drag those reluctant words onto the page. There are a ton of different things you can try to get the words flowing. One day, one thing will work, and the next time, something different might work. The important thing is to take action!

One thing that can really help is to change where you're writing. Go to a coffee shop or lie in a hammock. It's amazing how a new setting can loosen up words!

## AUTHOR PROFILE:

### Marilyn Singer

New York poet Marilyn Singer was a high school English teacher. One day she wrote a story at the Brooklyn Botanic Garden, and she followed that with lots of imaginative, award-winning books and poetry. She says, "I really love writing poetry and challenging myself, so who knows what wacky idea I'll have next?" When she's not writing, Marilyn is usually laughing or dancing.

## BODY ART

No season stamps me like summer—
with suntan and sand,
mosquito bites and streaks of sweat,
seaweedy speckles, scores of freckles.

As August ends, I muse
　on just how much I'll miss
these annoying or appealing
temporary tattoos.

# Look Around

## (It's Like I've Never Seen a Jelly Bean Before!)

Lots of poetry is descriptive. Look closely—at a chain link fence, your guinea pig, or a red jelly bean. Try taking a magnifying glass with you on a little poetry field trip. Study something small. What does it look like, sound like, feel like? How can you make your reader think, "I will never look at a jelly bean the same way again!"?

YOUR TURN

Pick a nearby object and write a poem from its point of view. Tell the object's secrets in the poem. For example, if you are a stapler, what could you confess? Maybe your stapler will say: *I have a bad habit of biting / My metal jaws snap at paper!*

## AUTHOR PROFILE:

### Nikki Grimes

*"I wouldn't call myself lucky, because hard work and perseverance form the bedrock of my success."*

–Nikki Grimes, *author of* Words with Wings, Planet Middle School, *and more*

California poet Nikki Grimes gave her first public poetry reading at age 13. Her New York City childhood included foster homes, dangerous neighborhoods, and too many schools to remember. Writing helped her cope, and she began publishing her poems while still in school. She has since written many award-winning poetry books.

## YOUR TURN

Nikki Grimes used writing to cope with hard situations as a teen. What's something hard you've faced? Write an "I Am From . . ." poem, sharing about the places, people, and events that have shaped you. Include at least a couple of challenges you've dealt with. For instance:

## I AM FROM . . .

I am from scorching Julys in my lungs
and seashells between my toes.
I am from lonely holidays and
cousins never known.
I am from a small, silent family
with many rules and few hugs.
I am from dreams of snow and song
and books for best friends.

# Excavate Your Idea Notebook

## (I Knew I Kept These for a Reason)

Don't forget to check in on your idea notebook (or file, or whatever) regularly. Those ideas won't do you any good if you never go back to them!

> "I do, however, keep a 'notebook' 'in the cloud.'... I always make time to jot down every poetical idea at the moment it pops into my head. Then when I find I have time to write, I rummage through this treasure trove of ideas for one that I would like to work on and develop."

–Kenn Nesbitt, U.S. Children's Poet Laureate, 2013-2015, *author of* ***The Armpit of Doom***, ***I'm Growing a Truck in the Garden***, *and more*

# Try a Poetic Form

## (Are You in the Mood for a Cinquain?)

Do you have a topic in mind but you don't know how to start? Choose a poetic form! Suppose your topic is the last school dance. Here are some possible first steps:

### HAIKU

Think about arriving at the dance and getting out of the car. Show that scene in a haiku, using a word that tells the reader what season it is.

### ACROSTIC

Write DANCE down your page. Brainstorm words about the dance: who you hung out with; the music; dancing or standing and watching; your clothes; the best moment; the worst moment, etc. Start matching up words and phrases with the letters you wrote down the page.

### CINQUAIN

Choose your first two-syllable line. How can you introduce the dance? Epic? Funny? Flailing? Lonely? Perfect?

### RHYMING FORM

Brainstorm words about the dance and list rhyming words for those key words.

# Chapter 6

# Make It Better!

## What Do You Mean, I'm Not Finished?

Growing a poem is like growing a plant. You start with a seed, or an idea. You plant it by writing a first draft. Then you feed it what it needs to grow. For a poem, that's time and revision.

You might focus on a different element, like sound or meaning, in each revision. With each draft, your poem will get leaner, stronger, better. How many drafts will you need to do? Some writers do three or four drafts. Others do many more. Basically you revise until you feel like the poem says what you want it to say in the best way you can say it.

You can use these revision techniques for any kind of poem: rhyming, free verse, haiku, acrostic, etc. Revising a rhyming poem takes longer, because you still have to make sure the right words rhyme and that the rhythm is the way you want it. But that's okay. Give yourself time to revise. Your poems deserve it!

# Take a Break

## (The Easiest Part of Revision)

We start by doing . . . nothing!

The crucial first step of revision is letting your poem rest. Put it away for a week, or maybe even one month. This resting time lets you read with new eyes and makes your poem's strengths and weaknesses easier to spot when you read it again.

But don't stop working. While one poem rests, brainstorm ideas for other poems. Write a new poem. Revise a poem that's already finished resting. There's always something you can work on.

# Revising for Word Choice

## (Words are Easy. Great Words Take More Work.)

Nikki Grimes on poetry:

"If it's done well, no words are wasted or minced. . . . I love that poetry can make a beeline for the heart."

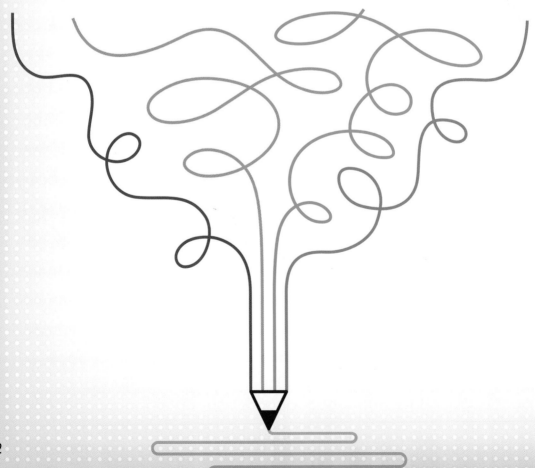

Fill your poem with specific, surprising words. In her haiku, Kelly Ramsdell Fineman uses "birches" instead of "trees." That helps the reader see the tree. Surprising words make poems remarkable. Fineman uses "gossip" where you might expect "whisper." How do you add surprise? One idea is to pick a random word to add to your poem. Random words are everywhere. Try these for inspiration:

- Your word box (shoebox filled with paper scraps showing words you love)

- A book or dictionary—shut your eyes and point, or flip through until one catches your eye

- The names of colors of paint or nail polish

A random word forces you to find new relationships between words. Maybe you'll create a startling image like the "liquid moon" in William Carlos Williams' "Winter Trees." Try it! Your results will vary from tragic to magic, and that's what makes it fun.

# Read Aloud

## (Where People Won't Look at You Strangely)

Poetry is read aloud more than any other literary form. Reading your work aloud as you revise is critical. Your poetry should flow—it should be easy to say out loud, without stumbling over words or phrases. It should sound good and be fun to say.

So shut your door and read your lines aloud as you try out different words. Choose words that sound good and add musicality to your poem.

# Revising for Meaning

## (Did You Say What You Meant to Say?)

Poets say things in new and interesting ways. That's part of poetry's magic. But you also want your meaning to be clear. There's only one way to make sure your poem says what you want it to: share it with some trusted friends. Ask them, "What happens in this poem?" Or "What is this poem about?" If their answer isn't what you expect, you can work on your poem to make it clearer.

It can be hard to hear that part of your poem isn't quite working. Just remember that they are not telling you that your poem isn't good. They're just asking questions or pointing out trouble spots in your writing. It's not personal. Listen. Then work on other projects for a little while. Later, reread your poem. Do their comments ring true now? Often you'll see things you hadn't noticed before and can work to make your poem even better.

# Chapter 7

# Sharing Your Work

## Shout It Out or Keep It Secret

Sharing a poem is kind of like cutting a piece of your heart out and projecting it on a big screen. Is it terrifying? Sometimes, but you are sharing something important—something that can only come from you. That can be powerful.

If you're nervous, start small. Give a copy of a poem to one person. Is your best friend having a rough day? Slip a funny verse story into her locker. Seeing how your writing affects other people is amazing. Their reactions can motivate you to write more, which will help you become an even better poet.

What if you're really private? Or your poems are too personal to share? That's totally fine. Writing poetry can help you sort through your feelings and process big things in your life. Your work is as valid and important to you as the poems of someone who can't wait to read her poems to the whole school.

If you can, take the leap. Text your poem. Tweet it, message it, share it! And share yourself. If you can't or don't want to, know that your poems are still a gift, even if they're a gift for only you.

# VOICE

Expressing unspoken thoughts
and burning desire,
a voice that is not part of the narrative
pauses for a breath;
the essential commands
and
extreme situations
still seem confusing.
Don't get discouraged.
Slow down,
evaluate your work,
and take your time
through talent,
steely focus,
and faith
to change the world.

–Matt Forrest Esenwine, all rights reserved

**YOUR TURN**

What is the thing you are most afraid to do? Stand up for a bullied classmate? Ride a roller coaster? Tell a friend she has hurt your feelings? Write a free verse poem that encourages someone to do that very thing that scares you.

# Join Other Poets

## (Power to the Poets!)

If you're new to sharing your work, team up. Joining up with other poets is always fun. Maybe you can share poems:

- in the morning announcements

- in the yearbook or school paper

- on posters in the cafeteria

- at special school events

- in printed programs for school plays or recitals

- at talent shows

- in the public library

- with seniors at a nearby senior housing complex

- at a teen open mic night at a coffee shop

Teaming up makes sharing less intimidating. Plus, you'll get to meet and hang out with other people who love poetry. Win-win.

# Publish Your Poems

## (When You Want to Make It Official)

Maybe you're hoping to do something more official, such as publish your poems. You have a couple of options—self-publishing (meaning you publish them yourself) or submitting to a magazine or newspaper that publishes poetry.

Self-publishing poetry is pretty easy in this high-tech world. If you have access to a computer and printer, you're set. Choose your best work, ask a friend who's good at grammar to proofread it, and add some nice design touches. Then, print out 20 copies of your poetry collection to share with family and friends.

You can also explore outside publishing possibilities. If you search online for "teens" and "poetry contest," or for "teen poetry submissions," you'll find contests and magazines that publish teens' poems, either in print or online. Ask a parent or teacher to make sure the contest is legit. You shouldn't have to pay an entry fee or pay for a copy of a magazine or book in which your poem is published.

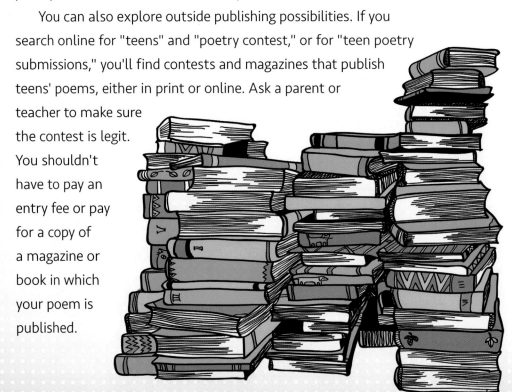

Here are a few tips for submitting your work:

- Send only your best poems.

- Include your name and contact information.

- Read the directions carefully and follow them to a T.

- Once you send off your work, start writing something new!

Hopefully, you feel ready to try new topics, new forms, and new approaches. When you look back over poems you've written, you'll probably find some that are ok, some that are embarrassingly bad, and one or two you absolutely love. That's awesome! It's like soccer. It takes a thousand drills to create one game-winning goal. So get out there and keep writing!

# Glossary

**accented** (AK-sent-ed)—a stressed syllable, which is spoken with emphasis

**acrostic** (uh-KROS-tik)—a poem that reveals a word or phrase when you read the first letter of each line down the left margin of the poem

**alliteration** (uh-lit-ur-AY-shun)—a beginning sound repeated in two or more words

**assonance** (ASS-O-nance)—a vowel sound repeated in two or more words

**book spine poem**—a poem created by stacking books so that the titles create a poem when you read from the top down

**cinquain** (sin-KANE)—an unrhymed 5-line poem with 2, 4, 6, 8, and 2 syllables

**collection** (kuh-LEK-shuhn)—book that contain poems by one poet

**consonance** (KAHN-so-nance)—a consonant sound repeated in two or more words, e.g., "bat," "chatter," and "written"

**Fibonacci** (Fib-o-NACH-ee)—a non-rhyming poem in which the number of each line's syllables equals the two before it

**found poem**—a poem created from words or phrases found in another text

**haiku** (hi-KOO)—a brief, non-rhyming poem capturing a moment in nature usually in a specific season

**internal rhyme** (in-TUR-nuhl rime)—when words within a single line or different lines rhyme with each other

**inverted** (in-VUR-tuhd)—taken out of its usual order

**meter** (MEE-tur)—the beat or rhythm of a poem

**near rhyme**—words that sound similar, like "grass" and "mash"

**perfect rhyme**—words that end with the same sound, like "wall" and "call"

**poetic forms**—different kinds of poems that have set rules to follow

**repetition** (rep-i-TISH-un)—when a word or phrase is used more than once

**revision** (re-VIZ-un)—the process of rewriting a poem to make it stronger

**sensory** (SEN-sur-y)—having to do with the five senses

**unaccented** (un-AK-sent-ed)—a syllable that is not emphasized

# Read More

**Janeczko, Paul B.** *Seeing the Blue Between: Advice and Inspiration for Young Poets*. Boston: Candlewick, 2002.

**Oliver, Mary.** *Rules for the Dance: A Handbook for Writing and Reading Metrical Verse*. New York: Mariner Books, 1998.

**Paschen, Elise, and Dominique Raccah.** *Poetry Speaks Who I Am: Poems of Discovery, Inspiration, Independence, and Everything Else*. Naperville, Ill.: Sourcebooks Jabberwocky, 2010.

# Internet Sites

Use FactHound to find Internet sites related to this book.
All of the sites on FactHound have been researched by our staff.

Here's all you do:

Visit *www.facthound.com*

Type in this code: **9781491459904**

# Index

# About the Author

Laura Purdie Salas has been writing poetry for more than 15 years. Her how-to book, *Picture Yourself Writing Poetry*, was on the International Reading Association's 2012 Teachers' Choice List. She has won a Eureka Gold Medal, NCTE Notable, and Minnesota Book Award for her collection, *BookSpeak! Poems About Books*. Laura lives in Minneapolis, Minnesota.